DEMOCRACY is the most used and most over worked word in the English language, used by Presidents, Prime Ministers, Leaders of Countries, and, Politicians in the World today. Essentially, used, by them, to manipulate, and to deceive.

All, claim, that they are democratic and, their country, is a DEMOCRACY; yet, so few of them have any real conception, of the true meaning of the word:

"The Right of the People to Govern Themselves"

DEMOCRACY
Government, Of, the People; By, the People; For, the People".

Sadly, due to the criminal negligence in regard to how they were taught and, the crass failure of the educational curriculum they endured; the majority of the ordinary 'common' people of Great Britain; have never been instructed how to properly, PARTICIPATE IN DEMOCRACY.

This book therefore is an essential guide for the British people, providing them with the information that they should know in order to participate.

The guide is set out in two parts: the first part posing the questions they ought to know; the second part providing the questions, and, the actual answers, that they should have known.

I suggest each British reader should try and answer the questions posed, first; before looking at the answers. In that way they will properly understand how badly let down they were, when they were being taught, during their education.

Good reading; best wishes, here's hoping for your better, awareness, and, for your better political and, democratic, participation; in the future.

Gordon J Sheppard

BRITISH DEMOCRACY...

Test for the People, verifying, that they are able to participate.

If you cannot answer these questions, you are unable to participate.

And, in consequence, Britain cannot be a Democracy. Because, if you do not know these answers; you, cannot know, what, Democracy, is.

This test determines whether you know how to participate properly in, BRITISH DEMOCRACY:

Question 1.

The American People have the, protection of law, provided for them, in a 'Written Constitution', 'Bill of Rights', and, the right of access, to a "Supreme Court of Law".

What, in comparison, do the British have in order to provide them with the same protection?

Question 2.

The British people elect their Parliament in General Election.

When a Parliament is elected at present, is it a democratic 'people's parliament'?

Answer 'yes' or 'no'? And, explain how and why.

Question 3.

Parliament has an office and a procedure known as the 'WHIPS'

What are the 'WHIPS'?

What do the 'WHIPS' do?

What the WHIPS do, is this legal?

Explain how and why.

Question 4.

The British Judiciary has always denied the people all right to challenge parliament in law.

How does the Judiciary deny this right?

Is that 'denial' lawful, or unlawful?

Explain how and why.

Question 5.

The British Parliament claims its "Supremacy".

How did parliament get this 'Supremacy'?

What is the 'Supremacy' for?

Does anything 'overrule' this "Supremacy"?

Question 6.

Each 'Reigning Monarch' sitting on the throne is provided with two legal instruments which enable them to do 'something important' in respect to parliament.

What are these 'legal instruments' called?

What are they for?

One of these legal instruments is involved in a particular way with every Bill or Act passed by parliament.

Explain:

How it is used?

When was the last time this instrument was used?

Question 7.

It is very much believed throughout Great Britain, and, the British People have always been taught, that the most important thing about the 'Glorious Revolution' is that it provided Parliament with its "Supremacy".

But, is this the most important feature of the 'Glorious Revolution'?

What other more important features did it produce?

Question 8.
King James the Second was removed from the English throne.
Explain:
How and why?
What affect does this have on the present 'Reigning Monarch', of today?

Question 9.
In order for a country to be a true democracy certain criterion must apply.
What are these conditions?
Does Great Britain meet this criterion?
Explain how and why?

Question 10.
In the National Census of 2011 the total British adult population (being over the age of 20)
was declared to be 48,085,800.
Explain:
How many are there In the total membership of all the political parties, in the country?
Is it right that this tiny minority dominates and controls virtually every aspect of life, of everyone in the country?
How is this political party domination and control maintained?

Question 11.
If you vote in General Elections,
What do you vote for?
What should you be voting for?

Question 12.
What is the "Original Contract"?
Explain in full detail:
How it came about?
What is it for?

Question 13
The present coalition administration acting as government was not elected by the people at all.
Is this a lawful government?
If the answer is yes, explain the, 'legal instrument', by which this governing is lawful?

Question 14

As this present coalition administration was not elected by the people in general election, yet, is now governing;

Did the 'Reigning Monarch' have any responsibilities in this?

Did, Elizabeth the Second, have any responsibility to intervene?

END OF TEST

ANSWERS TO THE TEST FOR 'BRITISH DEMOCRACY'

The test determines whether you know how to participate properly in, BRITISH DEMOCRACY:

Here are the answers you should have known:

Question 1.
The American People have the, protection of law, provided for them, in a 'Written Constitution', 'Bill of Rights', and, the right of access, to a "Supreme Court of Law".

What, in comparison, do the British have in order to provide them with the same protection?

The British do not have the same protection of law that the American's have; but they should be afforded the 'protection of law' as provided by, the 'Reigning Monarch' sitting upon the British throne; as required; by the, 'Original Contract'. This 'contract' is unwritten, but it is fully entrenched in LAW, and, it requires all 'Reigning Monarchs', to act as Head of Government; to monitor parliament; in the interests of all Subjects of the Crown. The 'Reigning Monarch' is required to protect the people from the tyranny of the 'abuses' and 'prejudice' of parliament.

The British also have the protection of Law, provided by the provision of the over-ruling paragraph, "The Said Rights Claimed", set out in the "Bill of Rights 1689"; which instructs parliament that when it applies its "Supremacy", nothing should 'prejudice' the people.

Question 2.
The British people elect their Parliament in General Election.

When a Parliament is elected at present, is it a democratic 'people's parliament'?
Answer 'yes' or 'no'? And, explain how and why.

The answer is 'No'. The people in democratic general elections elect their political representatives to represent them in parliament; but, the majority of those elected, on being elected, accept and comply with the 'diktat' and instructions issued by their political party, WHIP; and, therefore, they give the priority 'allegiance' to their political party; in preference, to those that elected them.

Question 3.
Parliament has an office and a procedure known as the 'WHIPS'
What are the 'WHIPS'?
What do the 'WHIPS' do?
What the WHIPS do is this legal?
Explain how and why.

The political party WHIPS in parliament instruct Members of Parliament on how they must behave in Parliament, and, how they must vote.
This political party activity is wholly illegal.
It, 'prejudices the people', by over-ruling and supplanting all rightful influence placed upon those 'elected' Members of Parliament, by the Constituent.
This, flouts, breaches, and breaks the 'precedent of law', providing the protection of the people set out in, "The Said Rights Claimed", the, over-ruling paragraph of the entire "Bill of Rights 1689"; which determines that when parliament enacts it "Supremacy", nothing should prejudice the people.

This is that paragraph in the "Bill of Rights 1689":

The, "Said Rights Claimed":
"And they do Claime Demand and Insist upon all and singular
The Premises as their undoubted Rights and Liberties and
that noe Declarations Judgements Doeings or Proceedings to
the Prejudice of the People, in any of the said Premises, ought
in any wise to be drawne hereafter, into Consequence or
Example"

Question 4.
The British Judiciary has always denied the people all right to
challenge parliament in law.
How do the Judiciary deny this right?
Is that 'denial' lawful, or unlawful?
Explain how and why.

The Judiciary deny the people this right by incorrectly
reading and interpreting the "Bill of Rights 1689". The
Judiciary has always claimed and ruled that "Article 9" of
that Bill, protects parliament from all challenge from
within LAW; Article 9, reads as follows:

"That the Freedome of Speech Debates and Proceedings
of Parlyament ought not to be Impeached or Questioned
in any Court or Place out of Parlyament"

And, the Judiciary has always claimed and ruled that this
prevents all challenge to parliament in the Courts. But,
the correct reading and interpretation of the entire "Bill of
Rights 1689" reveals the existence within that Bill of the
paragraph "The Said Rights Claimed"; and, this
determines that anyone is free, in law, to challenge
parliament in the Courts; if, and, whenever, parliament
'prejudice the people'. (See 'The Said Rights Claimed'
provided in the answers to Question 3, above).

Question 5.
The British Parliament claims its "Supremacy".
Explain:
How parliament got this 'Supremacy' ?
What is the 'Supremacy' for?
Does anything 'overrule' this "Supremacy"?

The, GLORIOUS REVOLUTION and the CONVENTION (Parliament) of 1688 set up by Prince William of Orange, created a 'Rights Committee' in order that they could produce a list of 'rights' parliament required, of a King. Parliament did not want to have to put up with the same interferences that it had endured under the previous King. King James the Second; who the CONVENTION had removed from the throne. This 'Rights Committee' produced the "Bill of Rights 1689" which under "Article 9" provided parliament with its "Supremacy".

Parliaments "Supremacy" provides that the Freedom of Speech, Debates, and Proceedings of Parliament, are protected by law.

Parliaments "Supremacy" can be over-ruled, by the authority and, 'precedent of law', set out in the paragraph, "The Said Rights Claimed" within the "Bill of Rights 1689". Which provides, that anyone may challenge parliament if and whenever parliament, 'prejudice the people'. (See this paragraph, "The Said Rights Claimed" provided in the answer to Question 3, above).

Question 6.
Each 'Reigning Monarch' sitting on the throne is provided with two legal instruments which enable them to do 'something important' in respect to parliament.
What are these 'legal instruments' called?
What are they for?

One of these legal instruments is involved in a particular way with every Bill or Act passed by parliament.
Explain:
How?
When was the last time this instrument was used?

These legal instruments are: "The Royal Assent" and "The Royal Prerogative".
They are provided to the 'Reigning Monarch' and, they have been specifically designed for only one purpose, the protection of the "Crown's Subjects'. They have no other purpose at all.

One of these 'legal instruments' the "Royal Assent" is provided in order that, the 'Reigning Monarch'; whose duty it is to protect the Crown's Subjects; shall monitor parliament and the Bills and Laws created by parliament, in order to see whether they are created honestly and without corruption; granting the "Royal Assent" if they are in the interests of the country and the Crown's Subjects; refusing, the, "Royal Assent" if they are not.

The Royal Assent has not been refused since 11th March 1708, when Queen Anne refused it for a Bill for settling the militia in Scotland.

Question 7.
It is very much believed throughout our land, and, the British People have always been taught, that the most important thing about the 'Glorious Revolution' is that it provided Parliament with its "Supremacy".
But, is this the most important feature of the 'Glorious Revolution'?
What other more important features did it produce?

Parliaments "Supremacy" is not the most important feature provided by the "Glorious Revolution".

The most important feature of the 'Glorious Revolution' and the CONVENTION (Parliament) it created; is the paragraph within the 'Bill of Rights 1689' created by the 'Rights Committee'; for the protection of the people. This paragraph, "The Said Rights Claimed" over-rules all other 'Premises' of the Bill, including, even the "Supremacy" of parliament itself, whenever parliament 'prejudice the people'. This is the most important feature provided by the, "Glorious Revolution".

Question 8.
King James the Second was removed from the English throne.
Explain:
How and why?
What affect does this have on the present 'Reigning Monarch' of today?

KING JAMES the Second was removed from the throne by the CONVENTION (Parliament) of 1688 for, *"Breaking the Original Contract betwixt King and People"*. The CONVENTION ruled and determined that he had thereby 'abdicated' his duty and that thereby he had 'abdicated' the throne. The CONVENTION declared the throne was, Vacant. And, Prince William of Orange was offered the throne. He accepted, and, became the next King.

This decision of the CONVENTION affects not only the present 'Reigning Monarch' sitting upon the throne; but, also all other 'Reigning Monarch's' in the *"Line of Succession"* who would also occupy the throne. Because, the CONVENTION ruled in respect of the, *"Lineal Descent"*, that,

"The Contract is as binding upon the Successor as well as it was on the Deposed, if the Successor broke the Contract, they too can be Deposed".

Question 9.
In order for a country to be a true democracy certain criterion must apply.
What are these conditions?
Does your country meet this criterion?
Explain how and why?

In any country claiming to be a, DEMOCRACY, only one criterion applies:
A, GOVERNMENT AND A PARLIAMENT, WHERE THE PEOPLE GOVERN THEMSELVES.

DEMOCRACY; is, "Government of the people, by the people, and, for the people." All other forms of Government are naught, but, the Totalitarian Regime.

Question 10.
In the National Census of 2011 the total British adult population (being over the age of 20)
was declared to be 48,085,800.

Explain:
How many are there in the total membership of all the political parties, in the country?
Is it right that this tiny minority dominates and controls virtually every aspect of life, in the country?
How is this political party domination and control maintained?

The political parties in the country treat their Membership numbers as a 'State Secret' and, as highly confidential. Only the Labour Party immediately revealed these numbers when asked. The Tory and Liberal parties arrogantly refused to disclose. However, by diligent research it was ascertained that the total political party Membership in the country, was slightly less than, 400,000.

Is it right then, that this *'less than 400,*000', should dominate and control virtually every aspect of the life of the, very slightly less, than 48,085,800 adults in the land; this is wrong; and, it is positively obscene.

This domination and control of the political parties in and over our lives is unlawfully maintained by the activities of the political party WHIPS in parliament; political, activities, having no legality, at all.

Question 11.
If you vote in General Elections,
What do you vote for?
What should you be voting for?

In General Elections the people afforded the right and the privilege of voting; they should be voting in order to select their 'political representative' to represent them and their interests in parliament.

THEY SHOULD NOT BE VOTING FOR A POLITICAL PARTY.

Question 12.
What is the "Original Contract"?
Explain in full detail:
How it came about?
What it is for?

The 'Original Contract' is an unwritten contract; but, it is fully entrenched and established in Law. It derives from the long since distant days of the past, when there were many 'Lords' and 'Kings', constantly fighting each other for power and control. The, common people of the land, the, 'serfs', of that time; would give 'allegiance' to their Lord and Master, for the protection of their Lord and Master. And, when the British Monarchy was first formed this 'idea' was then adopted, as the requirement, upon a King.

"Allegiance is given to the Liege Lord, for the protection of the Liege Lord".

That, is the very basis and the, concept, of the 'Original Contract'.

What is it for? The 'Original Contract' is the requirement upon every 'Reigning Monarch', in the, 'Line of Succession', requiring them, to act as 'Head of Government; to, monitor parliament, in order to verify that the Laws and Bills passed by parliament have been created without corruption; and, that they are, in the interests of the country and its people. The 'contract' requires the 'Reigning Monarch' to protect, all the 'Crown's Subjects from the tyranny of the 'abuses' and the 'prejudice' of parliament.

Any, 'Reigning Monarch', failing to honour the, 'Original Contract'; ABDICATES THE THRONE. Precedent in law for this, is determined, by the fact, that KING JAMES II, a living and lawful King, was removed from the throne for this reason in 1688: *"Breaking the Original Contract betwixt King and People".*

Question 13
The present coalition administration acting as government was not elected by the people.
Is this a lawful government?
If the answer is yes, explain the 'legal instrument' by which this governing is lawful?

The true legality is very questionable; the People's vote in the general election of 2010 determined two specific things: (A), that no political party should have a majority in parliament; and, (B), that there should be: a, "Conservative led Minority Government".

The People, did not elect or choose a coalition government at all. But, the leaders of the political parties elected to parliament in that election, they determined, that they could 'ignore' the People's wishes; and, that they could then create a coalition administration, to perform as government; entirely on their own.

There is no 'legal instrument' anywhere in the Kingdom, that provides the legality for this travesty of denying the 'Peoples wishes' declared in a democratic general election.

Question 14
As this present coalition administration was not elected by the people in general election, yet, is now governing;
Did the 'Reigning Monarch' have any responsibilities in this?
Did, Elizabeth the Second, have any responsibility to intervene?

Each 'Reigning Monarch' is provided with the right of use of the "Royal Prerogative". Provided to them for the protection, of the people. This 'legal instrument' provides the 'Reigning Monarch' with three options:

1. To advise Ministers of Government.
2. To warn Ministers of Government.
3. Whenever the wishes of the people are in direct conflict with the actions of the legislators (parliament), to order the dissolution of parliament.

Therefore, in the aftermath of the general election of 2010, when the people's vote had determined that there should be a 'Conservative led Minority Government' and, the leaders of the political parties then decided, to 'ignore' the peoples vote, and, thence to proceed to create, a 'coalition administration', to act as government, entirely on their own; here was the stark vivid 'evidence' that 'Option 3' above, had been flouted. And, in such circumstances, it was the duty of the 'Reigning Monarch' to intervene. With the 'peoples wishes' being ignored and overturned, as declared in democratic general election, there was the evidence of the 'direct conflict with the actions of the legislators' and the 'Reigning Monarch' ought to have ordered the immediate dissolution of parliament. There would then have been a new and fresh general election to decide the government of the day.

END OF THE ANSWERS TO THE TEST.

DEMOCRACY – The remedy....

It can readily be seen from the information provided previously in this book, that the British are being governed not only very badly, but, illegally as well. And, that Britain today is not a, DEMOCRACY. So, where is the remedy?

The remedy is very simple: the British people must stop blaming Government, Parliament and Politician for all that they badly do; asserting, as they do, that politicians are only in the business of politics in order to gain advantage and wield much power for themselves. The British must stop blaming politicians, when in reality; **it is their own damned fault.**

The British are so politically ignorant and so politically apathetic today, that they tolerate the 'abuses' of parliament and politicians, every day; without doing a damn thing about it. They are so politically unaware and so politically apathetic that they have come to believe, that nothing can be done. And, this is terribly wrong. Because, there is something, that can be done.

What is necessary to be done is to destroy once and for all, the overwhelming domination and control of an 'elected' parliament, presently, being dominated by the political 'diktat' of the political parties. This 'unlawful' political party domination of parliament must be brought to an end. The British people in democratic General Elections 'elect' their political representative to represent them and their constituency in parliament. And, therefore, on being elected, parliament should be a 'People's Parliament'. Thus, the democratic parliament elected, is not the political parties parliament. It is, the people's parliament; and, the political parties should not have any right of 'domination' over it.

This domination and control of parliament by the political parties is wholly 'unlawfully' maintained within parliament by the Offices, Procedure and Practices of the political party WHIPS. Which, each week, issues political party 'diktat' and instructions to 'elected' Members of Parliament, as to how they should behave in parliament, and, on how they should vote. Thereby, overruling and supplanting all 'rightful influence' placed upon those 'elected' Members of Parliament, by the Constituents. In, consequence, this 'unlawful' activity creates the **'prejudice of the people';** which is wholly outlawed and breaches the, 'precedent of law', set out in the, **"Statute in Force/Bill of Rights 1689/The Said Rights Claimed".**

Parliament and its politicians, and, the political parties represented in parliament do anything they please in parliament, because, they believe, that they are, protected by law from any challenge of the people. They firmly believe that the "Supremacy" of parliament afforded to parliament by 'Article 9' of the "Bill of Rights 1689", provides this protection. And, this is always backed up by the British Judiciary, which has always denied, any challenge to parliament in their Courts.

Article 9 of the "Bill of Rights 1689" reads as follows:

"That the Freedome of Speech Debates and Proceedings of Parlyament ought not to be Impeached or Questioned in any Court or Place out of Parlyament."

Both parliament and the Judiciary interpret and believe this to be the, 'LAW', denying **all challenge to parliament;** without, there being, any other 'considerations', at all. And, this misinterpretation of the "Bill of Rights 1689", and, 'Article 9'; has led them to be believe that the "Supremacy of Parliament" is, unchallengeable, and therefore, wholly, **Supreme.**

However, both parliament and the Judiciary, in interpreting the "Bill of Rights 1689" and 'Article 9', in this way, and, denying the people's right to challenge their 'elected' parliament's, 'abuses' and 'prejudice', in the Courts; made a serious error in this interpretation, on two counts:

Firstly, that the entire "Bill of Rights 1689" and specifically 'Article 9' were only created by the CONVENTION (Parliament) of 1688, in order to protect parliament from the interference of a King. The, Bill, was never created or intended, to protect parliament, from the People.

Secondly, and, therefore, in order to protect the 'People', from, **any misinterpretation,** of the Bill; (as both parliament and the Judiciary do so now); the "Rights Committee" of the CONVENTION, who created the Bill, inserted the, 'protection of the people', within the Bill, where it is located directly below all the thirteen 'rights', parliament is claiming from the King.

This, 'protection of the people', is provided by the paragraph, **"The Said Rights Claimed"** which reads as follows:

The, "Said Rights Claimed":
"And they do Claime Demand and Insist upon all and singular The Premises as their undoubted Rights and Liberties and that noe Declarations Judgements Doeings or Proceedings to the Prejudice of the People, in any of the said Premises, ought in any wise to be drawne hereafter, into Consequence or Example"

It can readily be seen that this paragraph is the overall 'authority' of the entire "Bill of Rights 1689", because it specifically states within its text, that it has the authority over, **"any of the said Premises"**, of the Bill. This means that, **"The Said Rights Claimed"**, is the overall 'authority' of 'LAW', over everything, written within the Bill.

It therefore makes it abundantly clear by, 'precedent of law', that parliament may 'enact' or 'apply', **Article 9,** of the Bill, and claim its "Supremacy"; but, **only on the conditions**, as set out in, **"The Said Rights Claimed".** Which specifically instructs parliament that, in applying its "Supremacy", that, nothing that parliament does, should, **'prejudice the people'.**

It can therefore be seen that **"The Said Rights Claimed"** overrules and supplants the "Supremacy of Parliament" itself, whenever parliament, **"prejudice the people".**

And, so therefore, if the British people want to reform parliament; by ending the present domination and control of the political parties over, 'elected' parliament, as they do now; all that it is necessary to do is to force both, Parliament and Judiciary, to 'officially' recognize the present, EXISTING LAW, of "The Said Rights Claimed". Which, both parliament and the Judiciary so, conveniently refuse to recognize now.

The paragraph, "The Said Rights Claimed", in the Bill of Rights 1689, is as true, and, as valid in 'LAW' as the, "Supremacy of Parliament", itself. But, at present, both parliament and Judiciary choose to, 'ignore', it; relying only, on 'Article 9' to prevent the people's right, to challenge the 'abuses' of their 'elected' parliament, from within law.

Force both parliament and the Judiciary to 'officially' recognize **"The Said Rights Claimed"** verifies that the, **'prejudice of the**

people', is unlawful. And, immediately, the political party activities of the WHIPS in parliament, which, do 'prejudice the people', automatically comes to an end.

This would ensure that, every vote taken in parliament from thereon, would become a, FREE VOTE. Thereby, creating, a true, PEOPLE's DEMOCRACY.

The very simple 'remedy' to ensure, that, the, "POWER OF THE PEOPLE" rests where the 'rightful power', should properly lie.

DEMOCRACY – LAW,

The, 'Rule of Law' and, the, 'Protection of Law'

Sadly, in Great Britain today 'LAW' has no relevance or meaning at all. The country and all the people abandoned the true meaning and intent of 'LAW', a long time ago.

LAW today in Great Britain is looked upon by the 'elite' and the 'establishment' of Monarchy, Government, Parliament, and Judiciary, as it being something, that only the 'common people' must obey. Whilst, they, all of them, flout breach and break 'LAW' all of the time.

Today, the British even have a "Coalition Administration masquerading as Government" that was not 'elected' at all. The leaders of the political parties elected to parliament in the democratic General Election of 2010, in the aftermath of that election, they did not comply with the *'People's Vote'* declaration that, there should be a "Conservative led Minority Government'; instead, they determined, **unlawfully,** that they could create a different form of government, entirely on their own. And, in complying with this unlawful, 'idea', they seized the power to govern just like any totalitarian dictator, creating this present 'coalition administration', without consulting, with the people, at all. There is no **'legal instrument'** anywhere in the British Kingdom that, 'provides the legality', for leaders of political parties elected to parliament, to overturn, overrule, supplant, or, ignore, the people's wishes as determined by democratic General Election.

Today, the British Judiciary even overrules and supplants the verdicts of Juries; **ordering re-trials;** where, the Jury has decided that they cannot agree a unanimous verdict of all the Jurors, by establishing 'guilt', **beyond all reasonable doubt.** Yet, this is the essential criterion of all Juries to abide by, in every criminal trial. The, 'Trial by Jury', is one of the most fundamental freedoms and protection of 'LAW' that, all, under the 'subjugation' to the British Crown have, in order to protect them from unjustly being convicted of crime.

Every, Judge, at every criminal trial, is required to instruct the Jury, that they can only deliver a verdict of 'guilty' if all the Jury agree that, 'guilt', is established **beyond all reasonable doubt.** But, today in Great Britain, Judges are deciding that they can overrule the Jury's verdict; and, they determine, 'guilt', all by themselves. Thereby, ordering, **retrials.** The only time there is 'justification' for any Judge to order a retrial, is where there has been 'technical error or abuse of law' in the manner in which the Jury has determined its verdict. For, instance, if there was the clear and precise evidence that a Member of the Jury had been, 'got at'. Or, if there was clear evidence, that a Juror or Juror's had been 'influenced' by press reports or, by other matters, outside of the Court.

Today, the political party WHIPS and their political party domination and control of an 'elected' Parliament, issues instructions to Members of Parliament each week, without any legality at all. This political party activity does, **'prejudice the people',** and thereby flouts and breaches the 'precedent of law' set out in the, "Bill of Rights 1689"/ **"The Said Rights Claimed".**

Today, the British have a 'Reigning Monarch' sitting upon the British throne charged with the responsibility and duty to honour and comply with the "Original Contract" requiring the 'protection' of all

'Subjects of the Crown'; yet, throughout her entire reign, she has not provided any protection at all.

Today, the British are held in 'subjugation' to the 'Reigning Monarch; being required, to give allegiance to every 'Reigning Monarch', for as long as a Monarch shall reign. Yet, they receive absolutely **nothing** in return. The very concept of the "Original Contract" that, **"Allegiance is given to the Liege Lord for the protection of the Liege Lord",** means absolutely 'nothing' to the British Monarchy, today.

Today, the British need urgently to set up a huge 'national debate' exploring the true meaning of 'LAW'. Because, today, the vast majority of the British people do not have a clue, what 'LAW' truly is. And, it is because of this, that they are presently dominated and controlled by the political parties; and, the, 'subjugation' to Monarchy, they now endure.

The British must determine once and for all what 'LAW' is.

This is best described by LORD HAILSHAM, an eminent ex-Lord Chancellor of England. When anyone asked him to explain what 'LAW' is, he would always reply saying this:

"LAW is a Myth, without the consent of the People, there is no LAW."

Thus, 'LAW' is naught but the voluntary consent of the People to live by the "Rule of Law".

Therefore, all that voluntarily give that consent to live by the "Rule of Law", are entitled to three specific things:

1. They are entitled to participate in the creation and framing of law.

2. They are entitled to 'equality' within law.

3. They are entitled to the 'protection' of law.

Yet, in Great Britain today, the People,, are denied all this.

They are denied the right to 'participate in the creation and framing of law' because, this is wholly dominated and controlled by the political parties in parliament, wholly controlled by the political party WHIPS.

They are denied the right to 'equality' in law; because both government and politicians constantly provides the advantages of, politically correct, 'positive discrimination' to the minorities; whilst heaping, **'negative discrimination',** against the majority. And. the 'elite' in the country dominates all. One only has to look at the front bench of the present coalition administration in parliament, to see how many were educated at, Eton.

The British today have no 'protection of law' whatsoever.

They have no, Written Constitution; or,

Bill of Rights setting out the proper rights and responsibilities of the people; or,

Supreme Court of Law, where it is possible to test, question, or even challenge the 'abuses' and the 'prejudice' of both government and parliament; from within law.

And, the 'Reigning Monarch' sits upon the throne; providing no protection at all.

The British, in truth and reality, do not endure their 'subjugation' depriving them of all of this protection of law; in order that the 'Reigning Monarch' shall act as patron or represent institutions and charities; or, host garden parties, or travel the globe promoting British good and British prestige; they endure their 'subjugation', depriving them of all the protection of law; because under the terms of the "Original Contract" each 'Reigning Monarch' sitting upon the British throne is charged with the responsibility, **to provide their protection of law.** And, the failure to do so, abdicates the throne.

Every 'Reigning Monarch' is provided with two 'legal instruments' wholly designed to protect the People. They are the **"Royal Assent"** and the **"Royal Prerogative'.** The 'Reigning Monarch' is required to act as Head of Government, to, monitor the Bills and Acts and the 'business of parliament', in order to see and verify there is no corruption; granting the **"Royal Assent"** if there is no corruption; refusing to grant it, if it is not in the interests, of the country, and, the people. The last time a 'Reigning Monarch' refused to grant the **"Royal Assent"** was on the 11th March 1708, when Queen Anne refused to grant it, to a Bill passed by parliament settling the militia in Scotland. Ever since that date, every 'Reigning Monarch' sitting upon the throne has granted the **"Royal Assent"** to every 'piece of paper' placed before them by parliament. They have miserably failed in their duty, to 'protect the Crown's Subjects, acting merely, as a village sub-postmistress or sub-postmaster, franking and rubber stamping everything presented to them by parliament.

The British are now expected to believe that every Act or Bill and all the 'business of parliament' since the 11th March 1708, has been conducted without corruption. And, this is ludicrous; hundreds of Bills have been created and passed by parliament under the influence of the WHIPS; and, the WHIPS in parliament have no legality at all. And, in our own lifetime, the British have recently witnessed the fraudulent Members of Parliament 'Expenses' fiasco; yet, the 'Reigning Monarch' did not lift a finger to intervene.

Each 'Reigning Monarch' sitting upon the throne also has the provision of the **"Royal Prerogative"** wholly created and designed in order to protect all 'Subjects of the British Crown". This legal instrument provides the 'Reigning Monarch' with three options: (a), to advise Ministers of Government; (b), to warn Ministers of Government; and, (c), whenever the peoples wishes are in direct conflict with the actions of the legislators, (parliament), to order the immediate dissolution of parliament.

Yet, when the leaders of the political parties in the aftermath of the 'People's Vote' of the General Election of 2010, determined that there should be a "Conservative led Minority Government', and, these leaders then seized the power to govern creating a coalition administration masquerading as government, entirely on their own; the, **wishes of the people** were flouted; and, here was the stark vivid evidence that the, **Wishes of the people were in direct conflict with the actions of the legislators;** yet, ELIZABETH THE SECOND, did nothing at all.. She should have immediately used the **"Royal Prerogative",** to order the immediate dissolution of parliament.

Oh yes; the British urgently need to organise a massive national conference and debate in order to determine once and for all,

THE TRUE MEANING AND INTENT OF 'LAW'

PARTICIPATION IN DEMOCRACY

DEMOCRACY, is, Government of the people, by the people, and, for the people.

It is not and, it never can be, Government and an elected Parliament wholly dominated and controlled by the political 'diktat' of the political parties. That is not, DEMOCRACY. That is, totalitarian tyranny, of the very worst kind.

Participation in, DEMOCRACY, is not the placing of an **'X'** on an election ballot paper once in every five years.

Participation in, DEMOCRACY, requires, the constant careful monitoring of Government, Parliament, Judiciary, and, all those that, **'rule over us',** twenty four hours of every single day; and, responding, actively in protest, when they do wrong. When, they depart, from the 'democratic actions and policies' that are determined by the 'free vote' of the peoples elected political representatives, "Members of Parliament"; and, then, replace this, by the political party 'diktat' of the, **Totalitarian Regime.**

If you want, DEMOCRACY,

You, must protect, DEMOCRACY.

Without the constant monitoring and protection of all of the people in a country, DEMOCRACY, is so very easy, to be abused.

Gordon J Sheppard

Bibliography:

"Declaration of Rights 1689".
Author: Lois G Schwoerer, Emeritus Professor of History, Columbia University.
Publisher: John Hopkins University Press.
ISBN: 0-8018-2430-3

"Parliamentary History of the Glorious Revolution"
Author: David Lewis Jones, ex Librarian, House of Lords, London.
Publisher: Her Majesties Stationery Office
ISBN: 11-701390 0

Statutes in Force – Bill of Rights
(1 Will. and Mar. Sess. 2.c.2)
Publisher: Her Majesties Stationery Office
Ref No. ABCD29:6:18

Author:

Name: Gordon J Sheppard

Date of birth: 16 May 1927

Born: At Watford, in the Country of Hertfordshire, England.

Education: Nil. Brought up, by a strict Roman Catholic family, taught by nuns and monks in Catholic schools, convents and monasteries; left school at fourteen years of age, knowing nothing. Could recite the entire Catholic Mass in Latin; but, beyond that; learnt virtually nothing. As, an adult, this has instilled a great desire for learning and, research. Try to learn something new every day.

Principal Interests: Politics, History, and, Law.

One day, very many years ago, I was so angry and incensed by a Bill passed by parliament, that I asked myself, **"Where is the true legality for the way I am being governed today? "** And, I then began the huge task to research this. After at least twenty years research, I have now to report, that I have found no legality at all.

My research into LAW, likewise, was most interesting. Researching the famous "Nuremberg Tribunals" that took place at the end of World War II, and, the trials of the various Nazi's accused of war crimes; it became apparent to me that although these trials are held up to be the very epitome of, 'Law and Justice'; in reality, they were wholly corrupt; because, all the Tribunal Judges, attempted, **"To put rain back in the Sky"**. These, corrupt Judges, attempted, to completely obliterate from their minds and, their, 'judgments', everything that had happened in Germany, since Adolf Hitler came to power. They actually determined that this, had not happened at all. In 'ruling' that, all the accused, could not claim that they were, **'only obeying an order',** in defence of their crimes; and, determining that, every defendant must be individually responsible for the crimes they committed; the Tribunal Judges, wholly ignored the law of the, **"FuhrerPrinzip"**. Shortly after Hitler came to power, 'Herman Goering', (President of the German State) created this law, which bound all the German Military to obey the order of a Superior Officer, under pain of death, if an order was disobeyed. And, during the war, this law was extended throughout the whole of Germany to bind every Civilian as well. People in Germany, were shot, heads were cut off by guillotine, and hundreds were sent to concentration camps, for disobeying an order or, for merely criticising the Nazi regime. **Nuremberg**, was, a travesty, of LAW.

Employment:

1958-1960: Works Manager and Director of, WEM (Watkins Electric Music) Company; specialising in the production of musical instrument equipment, guitars, amplifiers, and, organs, for the pop music industry.

Early 1960's: Promotions Manager for 'Radio London' the pirate radio station broadcasting from a ship at sea. Responsible for all 'on-shore' promotion and publicity activity, including all merchandising, and the mounting of discotheques, pop concerts, and, pop shows.

October 1973-May 1976: Promotions Manager for 'Capital Radio' the London first legal radio station licensed to broadcast continuous pop music every day. Where, responsibilities were exactly the same. Left Capital Radio in May of 1976 in order to start my own company producing souvenir merchandise for the 1977 Queen's Silver Jubilee.

May 1976: Managing Director, "Gordon Sheppard Promotions", creating and producing a range of 'Silver Jubilee' merchandise. Securing two 'Design Centre Awards', for a T-Shirt and, a Sweatshirt, judged by a panel of Judges headed by Prince Charles, deciding that they were among the best 'Silver Jubilee' souvenirs.

Other interests: Music: Classical Music, Great Choirs, and, Country music.

Status: Presently retired, housebound thru illness; badly swollen feet and legs.   11/07/2014

Notes:

Notes:

www.ingramcontent.com/pod-product-compliance
Lightning Source LLC
Chambersburg PA
CBHW070242290526
45789CB00004B/1723